YORKSHIRE TERRIERS

by Allan Morey

Consultant: Jennifer Zablotny
Doctor of Veterinary Medicine
American Veterinary
Medical Association

Pebble®
Plus

CAPSTONE PRESS
a capstone imprint

Pebble Plus is published by Capstone Press,
1710 Roe Crest Drive, North Mankato, Minnesota 56003
www.mycapstone.com

Library of Congress Cataloging-in-Publication Data
Names: Morey, Allan, author.
Title: Yorkshire terriers / by Allan Morey.
Description: North Mankato, Minnesota : Capstone Press, [2017] | Series:
   Pebble plus. Tiny dogs | Includes bibliographical references and index.
Identifiers: LCCN 2016006872| ISBN 9781515719663 (library binding) | ISBN
   9781515719724 (ebook (pdf))
Subjects: LCSH: Yorkshire terrier—Juvenile literature. | Toy dogs—Juvenile
   literature.
Classification: LCC SF429.Y6 M67 2017 | DDC 636.76—dc23
LC record available at https://lccn.loc.gov/2016006872

Editorial Credits
Emily Raij, editor; Juliette Peters, designer;
Pam Mitsakos, media researcher; Laura Manthe, production specialist

Photo Credits
iStockphoto: ktmoffitt, 4–5, Lisa Thornberg, 16–17; Shutterstock: alexkatkov, 21, Daz Stock, 7,
Iakov Filimonov, 11, kostolom3000, 3, back cover top left, Mr. SUTTIPON YAKHAM, cover,
9, rebeccaashworth, 12-13, vlastas, design element throughout book, Yevgen Romanenko, 1;
Thinkstock: dazb75, 19, Jaroslav Frank, 15

Note to Parents and Teachers

The Tiny Dogs set supports national science standards related to life science. This book describes
and illustrates Yorkshire terriors. The images support early readers in understanding the text. The
repetition of words and phrases helps early readers learn new words. This book also introduces
early readers to subject-specific vocabulary words, which are defined in the Glossary section. Early
readers may need assistance to read some words and to use the Table of Contents, Glossary, Read
More, Internet Sites, Critical Thinking Using the Common Core, and Index sections of the book.

Printed in the United States of America.
009656F16

TABLE OF CONTENTS

SPIRITED POOCHES

Yorkshire terriers are tiny.

But it seems they don't know it!

They are confident dogs.

People call these furry dogs

"Yorkies" for short.

People first bred terriers to hunt.
Small Yorkies chased after mice
and rats. Today Yorkies make
smart and spirited pets.

CUTE AND FEISTY

Yorkies stand about 8 inches

(20 centimeters) tall.

Most weigh less than

7 pounds (3.2 kilograms).

Yorkies' coats are long and silky. Their heads usually have gold or tan hair. The hair on their backs is often black or steel blue.

Yorkies are brave. They are not afraid of bigger dogs. They can even be aggressive toward other dogs.

Yorkies must be socialized as puppies. They need to spend time with other dogs. This helps them learn how to behave.

YORKIES AS PETS

Healthy Yorkies live up to 16 years.
They need special care.
Their long coats should be brushed
every day. Their hair should be
trimmed when it gets too long.

Like all dogs, Yorkies need some daily exercise. But they do not need a lot of room to run. They are great pets for people with apartments or small houses.

Yorkies love to be with their owners. They are sweet, loyal pets. Yorkies are happy to travel. Luckily, these small dogs are easy to take with you!

GLOSSARY

aggressive—strong and forceful

behave—to act properly

brave—showing courage and willingness to do difficult things

breed—to mate and produce young

coat—an animal's hair or fur

exercise—a physical activity done in order to stay healthy and fit

loyal—being true to something or someone

socialize—to train to get along with people and other dogs

spirited—full of courage and energy

terrier—a type of small dog originally used for hunting

READ MORE

Beal, Abigail. *I Love My Yorkshire Terrier.* Top Dogs. New York: PowerKids Press, 2011.

Edison, Erin. *You'll Love Morkies.* Favorite Designer Dogs. North Mankato, Minn.: Capstone Press, 2015.

Shores, Erika L. *All About Yorkshire Terriers.* Dogs, Dogs, Dogs. North Mankato, Minn.: Capstone Press, 2013.

INTERNET SITES

FactHound offers a safe, fun way to find Internet sites related to this book. All of the sites on FactHound have been researched by our staff.

Here's all you do:

Visit *www.facthound.com*

Type in this code: 9781515719663

Super-cool stuff! Check out projects, games and lots more at **www.capstonekids.com**

CRITICAL THINKING
USING THE COMMON CORE

1. Yorkshire terriers were originally hunting dogs. What traits do you think a good hunting dog needs for catching mice and rats? (Integration of Knowledge and Ideas)

2. Describe a Yorkie's coat. Do you think its coat needs more or less grooming than other dogs? Why? (Integration of Knowledge and Ideas)

INDEX